SEO

Proven Search Engine Optimization Strategies to Dominate Google

The author of this book has taken careful measures to share vital information about the subject. May its readers acquire the right knowledge, wisdom, inspiration, and succeed.

Table of Contents

Introduction 1

Chapter 1: Understanding SEO 3

Chapter 2: SEO Strategies 15

Chapter 3: Common Mistakes and How to Avoid Them 35

Chapter 4: Best Practices.. 47

Chapter 5: Putting It All Together 57

Conclusion 63

Introduction

Congratulations on purchasing this book and thank you for doing so.

The following chapters will teach you everything that you need to learn about SEO that will get your website or blog on the first page of Google search engine result pages.

Chapter 1 discusses the basics so that you will have a good foundation on what SEO really is.

Chapter 2 teaches the effective strategies that you can use to increase your website's SEO ranking. This chapter reveals the powerful keys that you need to increase your website's visibility.

Chapter 3 talks about the common mistakes that beginners make. It is important that you be aware of these pitfalls so that you will not commit the same mistakes.

Chapter 4 lays down the best practices followed by top SEO practitioners and successful bloggers.

Chapter 5 is about putting everything together and moving forward. After all, SEO is a lifelong practice. You should turn the SEO strategies and best practices into a habit.

There are plenty of books on this subject on the market, thanks again for choosing this one! Every effort was made to ensure it is full of as much useful information as possible. Please enjoy!

Chapter 1
Understanding SEO

SEO is an acronym that stands for *Search Engine Optimization*. It is a practice that aims to increase the visibility of your website or blog. By using the right SEO strategies, you will be able to optimize your website that it can easily be located by search engines. This will make your website or blog appear on the first page of Google and other search engines. As a result, it can lead a tremendous amount of traffic to your website or blog, which has the potential to be converted into sales.

Benefits of SEO

SEO is a must to apply these days. With countless of websites out there, there is almost no chance to get your website any form of visibility unless you know the best SEO practices. Here are the benefits of using SEO strategies:

- Increased visibility

    Of course, an obvious benefit is an increase in visibility. Your site can appear on the first page of Google, so more people can discover your website. This is the most common benefit of using SEO.

- More traffic

    As a natural result of being more visible, you can expect to get more traffic to your site. Hence, if you use your site to make a profit either through ads or by selling products or services, there is a good chance that you can increase your income by converting your traffic into sales. After all, no matter how wonderful is the product that you offer, you cannot expect to make any money with it unless people know about the existence of your business.

- Zero cost

  SEO costs nothing. As long as you know the best SEO strategies and practices, all that you need to do is to apply them. And, no, you do not need to purchase any software or tool. Of course, you still have an option to avail of paid SEO services, but it is not required. If you stick to the SEO techniques revealed in this book, you can have your website on the first page of Google within a few weeks.

- Practical

  If you are serious about driving traffic to your site, then you cannot ignore the use of SEO. Especially these days, the competition among different websites is tough. You need to use SEO to leverage your chances of success and get ahead of your competitors. Not to mention, your competitors are also using SEO strategies. Therefore, you need to apply the most effective strategies and apply them properly.

- Better than ads

  Many people believe that SEO is better than paying for ads. When you avail of ads, you need to pay each time a person clicks on your advertisement. You will have to rely on your ads just for your site to be found. However, the more you use these ads, the more your cost increases. This is not the same with SEO. Yes, SEO may take a longer time to get established than paid ads, but once you hit a good SEO ranking, things will be much easier, and you can enjoy significant benefits.

- Better exposure

According to a study, about 60% of people who search the web do not go past the first page of Google. So, what does this mean? If your site does not appear on the first page of Google, then you are losing a big amount of traffic to your site. To be on the first page of Google search engine result pages, you need to apply powerful SEO strategies. Again, your competitors also know about SEO. If you do not optimize your site for a search engine, then you will never get the exposure that you deserve.

- Better credibility

People trust Google. After all, when it comes to search engines, Google is a giant that people rely on. If your site appears on the first page of Google, then people instantly think that your website is reliable and can be trusted. However, if your site cannot be found on the first page of Google, people will hesitate as to whether to trust your website or not.

Website vs. blog

Is there a difference between a website and a blog? It is safe to say that there is no difference between the two. However, for the sake of all word Nazis out there who are so particular about the meaning of every terminology, there are a few things that may differentiate a website and a blog from each other.

On the one hand, a website is a more formal and static page. Business websites would be a good example. There is also little to no engagements involved. On the other hand, a blog is less formal and is usually updated with new contents on a regular basis. Unlike a website, blogs often allow and even encourage to have engagements with the readers via the comment box. A blog is a social media platform that is a bit more personalized and formal. Take note, however, that this book uses both terms (website and blog) anonymously. After all, all SEO strategies apply to both.

The importance of choosing the right topic, product, or service

It is important that you choose the right topic for your website. The reason is that maintaining a blog is a lifelong journey. You are expected to come up with numerous helpful contents. The best advice is to come up with a blog about something that you love. For example, people who love running come up with a site about running where they share their experiences, insights, tips, and tricks, among others. Those people who love to travel create a travel blog where they share their the do's and don'ts of traveling, as well as the places that they have visited. The first step to SEO is to have a specific subject to write about. After all, there is nothing for you to optimize for search engines if you have nothing to share.

Of course, you are also free to come up with a site that is not in line with your personal interests. There are webmasters and bloggers who do this just for the purpose of earning a profit. The problem here is that you will find it difficult to come up with unique and useful contents, and you might end up merely rewriting the contents of others, which is a bad practice that you should avoid. Your best option would be to hire a professional ghostwriter who truly understands the subjects and will write the contents for you. However, hiring a professional ghostwriter who produces high-quality works can be expensive, especially if you intend to hire him for a long term. Hence, for starters, it is best to stick to a topic that you know, something that you are truly interested in.

Quantity vs. quality

When asked about SEO, people always say that you should focus on the quality. Although this is a good advice, it is also not clear enough. When it comes to SEO, you need to focus on both quality and quantity. Yes, quantity is still important. In fact, Google will not even allow your blog to be eligible to post Google ads if you only have five posts, regardless of how high is the quality of your posted articles. Also, a reader would find it hard to recommend your site if it fails to tackle a subject completely. Since one article only focuses on a single topic, you need to have lots of articles on your site to cover and discuss your subject. There are writers who combine many topics in a single article which ends up with a confusing and low-quality article. Also, the more high-quality articles you have on your site, the better chances you have of being recommended by Google and other search engines.

How Google search engine works

An important part of learning SEO is to know just how Google search engine really works. It is worth noting that Google's search engine cannot be underestimated. It is a powerful and well-organized tool. Without it, it would be hard to find whatever you are looking for when you browse the worldwide web. Just like other search engines, Google also uses a special algorithm to find whatever it is that you are looking for. Now, Google does share some facts related to its special algorithm, but some of its specifics remain a secret. Such secrecy is important so that anyone who has such knowledge cannot abuse the system. This is to ensure that the articles on the first page of Google are worthy of being recommended. Otherwise, Google may lose the competition with other search engines.

Just like other known search engines, Google also makes use of automated programs, such as crawlers and spiders. It also has a huge index of collected keywords which can help identify the best articles to be recommended to those people who make a search online. What makes Google so much better than other search engines is how well it ranks the countless of articles in its system. This refers to the order of links or articles that you will find when you make a search online. Google ensures that the most relevant and best pages appear on the first page of its search results. Google uses what is known as PageRank. This assigns a certain score to every web page. The higher the score, the better is its SEO ranking, and the more chances it will get at appearing on the first page of Google's search engine results page (SERPS).

PageRank

Google's PageRank depends on four factors. Of course, when it comes to SEO, you cannot neglect the use of keywords. After all, the keywords are the main ingredients on how Google index or sort out its directory that will be transmitted to the SERP. It is important to take note of the location, as well as the number of times the keywords are repeated in an article or post. The number of times that your keywords should appear in a post, also known as the keyword density, will be discussed later in the book. Obviously, if you only repeat your keywords once in an article, then you can expect for that article not to rank well in search engine results. After all, keywords are meant to be repeated several times in a post.

Another factor is the time that the page has existed. Although search engines like Google prefer the freshest contents, it also takes into consideration those pages that have an established history. It is common to find pages that get deleted after a few months or years. Those posts that remain and have established a history are usually those that have a high quality and credibility. Of course, such pages have a higher chance of getting a good SEO ranking provided all the other criteria are met.

One of the most important things to consider is the number of pages that link to a particular post. The more web pages link to your site, then the better chances you have of getting a high ranking. But, this is not just about getting as many links as you can. Google is more developed today than before and only considers links from well-established sites. You may be wondering why links are given a big importance. The reason is that links from external sources are unbiased. When you write something yourself, it is easy to make it more meaningful or valuable than it is. After all, it is your creation. However, when viewed by a third party, the value of your work is seen as it really should be, without any bias and prejudice. If other webmasters use your post and link to it, then it is a clear sign and confirmation that your post is really worth being read and therefore should get a higher SEO ranking.

Last but not least, the quality of your articles is of utmost importance. Before, you can just stuff your articles with keywords and meet all the other criteria to get a good SEO ranking.

However, Google never stops to develop its system. Today, it is of utmost importance to provide high-quality and informative articles to make Google pay attention to your contents.

Spamming

Google also punishes sites that spam the system just to get a boost in SEO ranking. Spamming is counterproductive and usually results in removal from Google's index. How does Google handle a spam? It is worth noting that Google relies on mathematics. According to Google, spam is handled also by their special algorithm. Take note that Google's algorithm also includes human intervention.

Google does not respond immediately to spam reports. If you aim to just beat your competitors by reporting to Google about their activities that may be considered a spam, then you will be better off just working on your own site. After all, if there is really an activity that operates as a spam, Google's algorithm will surely be able to detect it and cause the site's SEO ranking to drop.

In case it is your site that has been reported for any spam activity, then you have to stay calm. Do not worry; in the event that the report was made due to automated spam penalty, your site will be back online after a period of 60 days from the moment that the cause which triggered the spam has been removed. However, if the spam report was made manually (your competitors may do this), then the penalty may take a longer period. But, do not worry; you can always send Google a reinclusion request. Just be sure to remove the cause of the spam before you send Google any message.

Google Analytics

If you are serious about dominating Google, then you should also use Google Analytics. It is your tool to measure and analyze the performance of your site. There are many benefits of using Google Analytics. It will provide you with helpful information, such as the number of visitors to your site, their location, the marketing strategies that drive the most traffic to your site, how to improve your site's speed and improve its performance, and the contents on your site that your visitors or readers like the most, among others.

The first step is for you to get a Google Analytics account. Do not worry; signing up is easy. If you already have a Google e-mail address, then you can use that e-mail address. If not, then it is time for you to create one. Take that the Google account that you use will serve as the admin of your Google Analytics. As such, it will have full control over it. Although you can soon grant access to other people, they will only be given limited access to your Google Analytics. Therefore, do not let someone else create a Google Analytics for you.

Setting up Google Analytics is easy. Just follow the instructions. You will be given a tracking code that you need to include in your site's HTML. This is to allow Google Analytics to read and analyze your website. You can then start viewing your analytics data from Google. Feel free to set goals and types of analytics report. You can use the information that you can get to help improve the SEO ranking of your website. The layout and features of Google Analytics are highly intuitive, so you would not have a problem with navigating it.

White Hat vs. Black Hat SEO

White hat SEO refers to legitimate SEO practices. As such, you can use it without having to worry about getting penalized by Google. Of course, the opposite is black hat SEO, which refers to SEO practices that are abusive and unsafe ways to boost the SEO of a website. Although some black hat techniques may work for some time, you can expect that Google will soon find out about them, and the consequences of using black hat SEO can be severe. Therefore, stay away from black hat SEO and stick to using only white hat SEO strategies.

Focus on a human audience

Take note that even after learning the different strategies to increase your site's SEO rating you must always take into consideration that you are dealing with a human audience. Some SEO practitioners get too aggressive and obsessed with the idea of tweaking the algorithm of Google just to be on the first page of the SERP. Although you may get lucky and be successful at this, you cannot expect to remain on the first page of Google for so long. To be safe, put your audience in mind. Never forget that your audience is composed of real people who want to see high-quality contents.

Avoid manipulative ways to improve your SEO. Such irregular and unfair practices are referred to as black hat SEO. Although they may work for some time, Google will soon shoot down those sites that employ black hat practices.

Chapter 2
SEO Strategies

It is now time for you to learn the different SEO strategies that will place your website on the first page of Google and other search engines. Take note that these strategies should be combined in order to get the best outcome.

High-quality contents

If there is one thing that you need to optimize your site, it is producing high-quality contents. But, what makes a content of high quality? There are certain standards that you need to meet in order to qualify your article to possess a high or professional quality.

The first thing that you need is to make every article informative. This means that every post that you make should be packed with useful information. People who search for things online often look for answers to specific questions. Your posts should be able to help and satisfy your readers that they no longer need to visit another website.

The next thing that you need is to be able to share such information in an effective way. This refers to your ability to convey your thoughts and ideas into words. Do not worry; you do not need to be a professional writer to come up with high-quality articles. In fact, there are many successful blogs out there that are not managed by professional authors. However, to be successful, you do need to have a decent writing skill. Your website visitors will find it difficult to take you seriously if your articles are full of grammatical and punctuation errors. No, you do not need to produce perfect articles, but they should be decent enough and presentable. It is recommended to use simple words and lines to convey your ideas.

Take note that the quality of your articles should be compared with the quality of the articles written by your competitors. After all, even if you consider a particular article to be informative, it is still not informative enough if your competitors have articles on the same topic with more information.

A good way to learn how to write high-quality articles is by visiting and reading the contents of famous websites, blogs, and magazines. The more you examine and analyze how their articles are written, the more you will get an idea of the right flow and structure of your own articles.

Long-tail keywords

When it comes to SEO, the key is the use of keywords. To increase your SEO rating, you need to repeat these keywords a certain number of times in an article. Take note that the people who make a search online only key in keywords in the search bar. If you are able to match these keywords and offer high-quality contents, then you can significantly increase your chances of being recommended by Google.

Gone are the days when you can just use one or two keywords. Since there are now so many online articles that have been written on the same subjects, you need to be more specific.

Today, the recommended practice is the use of long-tail keywords. Long-tails keywords are composed of three or more keywords. For example, you do not just use the keyword, Mike Tyson, if your article is about his training regimen. After all, there are countless of articles on the world wide web that contain the name of Mike Tyson. Instead, you should be more specific. You may use the keyword phrase, Mike Tyson training program, as effective long-tail keywords.

Keyword density

Keyword density simply refers to the number of times the keywords are repeated in an article. Various experts have concluded that there is no hard and fast rule as to the best keyword density. However, the majority recommend keeping the keyword density somewhere between 1% to 3% per article.

Keyword placement

People advise that your keywords should appear several times in an article. But is there any advice as to where in the article they should appear? Yes, it is recommended that your keywords should at least appear in the title, in the beginning paragraph of your article, in the middle of the body of your article, as well as in the last or concluding paragraph. With your keywords strategically scattered in these places, there will be a better chance that Google will recognize them. Stuffing your keywords all together in one paragraph will make it seem to Google that you are merely engaged in the bad practice of keyword stuffing, which can cause your SEO ranking to decline.

Google keyword planner

When you write an article, there is simply so many keywords that you can think of. So, how do you know the best one to use? You can use Google keyword planner. To use Google keyword planner, you first need to sign up for a Google Swords account. Do not worry; signing up is fast and easy. And what is more, you do not have to pay anything to create an account. Just visit Google Adwords website and follow the instructions.

Once you have an Adwords account, you can now access Google keyword planner on the Adwords platform.

When you use Google keyword planner, you will be able to know how many hits (web searches) are made using a particular keyword or keyword phrase within a specified period of time. You can also sort the results according to geographical location, language, and others. Not only that, Google will also provide you with keyword suggestions so that you will be able to use the best long-tail keywords available. The good news is that all these are free of charge.

Take note not to count the results for generic keywords, such as a mere name of a famous person. Just because a particular keyword phrase gives you a high number of hits, it does not automatically mean that there is a good market for your chosen keywords. Again, use long-tail keywords and be more specific as possible.

Google Adwords

Google Adwords is the platform that will allow you to post Google ads (your ads) for a fee. This is also an effective way to increase your SEO because it will lead real and high-quality traffic to your site. This is better than those paid services online that promise to direct thousands and millions of traffic to your site because such traffic only comes from bots and fake accounts, which is bad for SEO. Once Google detects that you use such "cheat" to generate traffic (and it will), it will stop recommending your site which will lower your SEO rating. Another advantage of using Google Swords is that you are assured to get your money's worth. Take note of this: You will only be charged a fee every time somebody clicks on your advertisement. You do not have to pay for impressions or mere views of your advertisement. This is also a quick and easy way to have a link to your site on the front page of Google search engine page results.

Page title

Your page title, also known as the title element, is one of the most important factors to consider for SEO purposes. It is also what is used by Google as a snippet in a search result. It is recommended that your keywords should also appear in your title. It is a common advice to make your title catchy and interesting. However, just remember that your title must be relevant and must state directly what the contents of the article are about. After all, the main purpose of a title is to give to the reader an idea of what the article is about and not solely for the purpose of increasing the SEO ranking of a site or blog.

Optimize for a long click

A long click is where a person clicks on a link in the SERP and spends time with the resulting page. Sometimes he even abandons to make other searches. This, of course, relates to user experience and satisfaction. Long clicks are good for SEO. It shows that you have a quality site. Of course, to do this, your site must be professionally designed and has high-quality posts. This is also the reason why your homepage and every page on your site should be well structured and written. You need to convince your reader to stay on your site for a longer period of time.

Catchy opening paragraph

Most readers do not really finish reading the whole article. If the first few sentences of an article are not compelling enough, they will tend to hit the back button and check another site. Therefore, it is important that you make the introductory statement of your articles compelling enough. Otherwise, your readers will even fail to reach the middle or body of your articles where the real details can be found. Just like any advice in article writing, make the beginning paragraph compelling enough that it will trigger the interest of your reader to find out more of what is written.

Link building

To achieve a website that ranks well in search engines like Google, link building is one of the most helpful strategies that you can use. It is worth noting that you do not really force people to link to your site. However, you can persuade other webmasters to link to your site. To do so, you need to share something that is valuable that your readers would want to share it with their own network. Again, having high-quality contents is the key.

Do not just focus on contents that are good for monetization purposes. Take note that all your contents function as a single unit since they are all found on the same website. If one of your contents do well and get more interactions with readers, then your other contents also get promoted indirectly, but effectively.

You can also participate in topical hubs and forums. You should get involved in the discussion so that you can get a good amount of attention. Of course, you should only do so discreetly and professionally. Another way to draw link building is by commenting on other relevant sites. You should also be updated on the news. If your topic and content can help resolve a current issue or at least shed some new light on the issue, then it may be an article that many webmasters would find interesting to link to.

Establish your expertise

To dominate Google, it is important that you establish your expertise over your niche. You should be the go-to person when it comes to topics about your niche. Of course, it takes time to build a name for yourself and to be considered as an expert, but it is possible. In fact, it should be a priority. The top sites are those that have well-established names in their respective niches. And, no, you do not need to be the number one expert, but at least be among those that are considered as experts. Part of establishing your expertise is to connect with leading experts on the subject. Take note that if you are connected with experts, then it will be easier for you to soon identify yourself or your site to be on the same level as the other experts. Needless to say, it is important that you provide useful and informative contents. Otherwise, no reader will treat you seriously as an expert. Sometimes it is also a matter of how you present yourself that is important. People will never view you as an expert if you are unprofessional and only shares basic information found on other sites.

You might be wondering: Can you still be an expert even if you are not personally knowledgeable about a particular topic? Well, the answer is yes, you can still *appear* to be an expert. After all, you can always research any subject and come up with remarkable conclusions. However, real expertise means so much more than researching. It takes devotion and practice. There are many people online, such as those who claim to be experts when it comes to investing in stocks, who are not real experts but only market themselves as an expert on the subject. Beware of these people. And, as much as possible, do not be like them.

Be unique

If you are planning to put up a site so that it will be like an already existing website, then forget about it. Google does not like duplicate contents. Even before you start a website, think of a way to make it unique. It is this uniqueness that will be your strength amidst the tight competition. If you cannot offer anything new, why would Google give you a high SEO ranking?

Take note that being unique does not mean that you should write about something that is totally out of this world. Rather, being unique means giving a new voice to the same thing. Sometimes a shift in perspective is all that you need to do this.

Social media marketing

You should learn to use social media to your advantage. Now, there are many social media platforms to choose from. The most recommended are Facebook and Twitter. If you are not fond of social media, you can just choose one platform to promote your site.

Social media is the way to get your contents to go viral on the Internet. Of course, it is an effective way to boost your SEO. Just be sure that you have articles posted on your blog that you can be proud of.

You can use social media to promote your site by sharing links that will direct your followers or connections to a particular post on your blog.

Optimize your domain name

Be careful how you choose your domain name. It is the name that your site will be known in the Internet universe, so choose it wisely. You also cannot change your domain name, so be careful and give it some time when you decide what name you will use.

It is recommended that you use a name that will reflect what your website or blog is about so that the people who learn the name of your site will know what to expect when they visit it. Of course, if the name also implies something that they are interested in, then there is a good chance that they will check it out. You may want to use a generic word to be part of your blog so that people will easily have an idea what your site is about. For example, if your site is related to the health niche, then you may want to use a word that is related to that specific niche, such as body, health, medicine, or remedies. Of course, this rule is not absolute. There are also many successful blogs with high SEO that do not use a generic word. For example, many professional authors simply use their full name as their domain name. Some successful blogs use three or four seemingly random letters. However, for starters, it is best to stick to the usual recommended practices.

Own a niche

You need to specialize in a particular niche. This will be your subject expertise. Taking on a topic that is too general is no longer a good choice since people want sites that display mastery of a particular subject.However, do not make your site be too specific that it will be difficult for you to come up with new articles.

Once you have chosen a niche, be sure that every article that you post belongs to your chosen niche. Do not follow the practice of other bloggers who suddenly branch out to another niche. It is also good for your site's SEO to repeat certain parts of the keywords that you use among your articles.

Does focusing on your niche really a way to boost your SEO? Not necessarily, however, it is an effective way to make your blog visitors and readers trust your site, which is important not only to SEO but to the overall development of your site.

Add ALT texts to images

Using images is good. Most people get intimidated when they see a website that is full of nothing but texts. Images can make your contents look more interesting. However, when it comes to SEO, you should know that Google will not be able to "read" or understand any images that you upload unless you apply ALT texts to them. ALT texts refer to the small description that you can commonly find below an image. It is this short description that will enable Google to understand what an image is about and can give it a higher SEO ranking. Therefore, the next time you upload an image, be sure to add ALT texts. It is also good to use your keywords as part of your ALT texts.

Engage with your readers

If you manage a blog, do not forget to add a comment box where you can engage with your readers. Although this will not increase your SEO directly, this practice is an effective way to draw regular and new followers to your blog or site.

If you do not want to have engagements on the site itself, then you can choose to engage with your readers via social media. The more active is your level of engagements, the more chances you have of getting more likes and reshapes, as well as more followers. All these, of course, will increase your overall SEO rating.

Site audit

The purpose of a site audit is to ensure that the site is functioning at its best performance. It is also a way to check for any improvements that you can make. From time to time, you should check the external links in your articles are still working properly. It is not uncommon for links to be broken after a few months or years, especially if the website that you are linking to undergoes an update. You should also take this opportunity to read and edit your articles. It is normal to overlook some mistakes, especially issues with grammar and punctuation. Also, make sure that every page on your site is functioning well and can upload quickly. If the size of images becomes a problem, you might want to use JPEG images over PNG images.

Guest posting

Guest posting is one of the best ways to draw traffic to your site, as well as to get backlinks from well-established websites. But, first, what is a guest post? It is where you post an article on another person's blog or website. It is worth noting that not all websites accept guest posts, just as you are free to accept or not to accept first posts on your own blog.

So how do you know if a particular site accepts guest posts from other people? Well, normally, the site itself will announce it on one of its pages. Such sites will usually have an editorial guideline as part of its Contact page. It may also have a Write for Us page. If the site does not offer a way to submit an article or a query letter, then there is good chance that it does not accept guest posts. A quick way to recognize if a site accepts articles from other people or writers is by checking the authors on the site or blog. It the site has multiple and different authors, there is a good chance that it accepts guest posts. The best way to find out is by sending a message to the site's admin or editor via the Contact page.

Internal links

It is a good practice to use internal links to your articles. An internal link is where you highlight (clickable link) a particular word or set of words in your article that's linked to another article that you have written. This is a good way to suggest and guide your readers as to what to read next.

Optimize your homepage

Your homepage is the center of your website. This is what people will see when they access your main domain URL. Ideally, your homepage should have all the important keywords related to your site. This is to draw as many traffic as possible. The more related keywords and high-quality articles that you have, the better is your chances of succeeding.

Design and layout

Part of working on your site's SEO is providing the best possible reading experience. Therefore, your site should be professionally designed. Take note that your blog visitors will not be able to read and appreciate your contents if the design and layout of your blog do not persuade them to read further. Therefore, having a professionally-designed blog should be a priority.

What makes a professional design and layout? There is no hard and fast rule on this subject. Depending on the platform that you use for your website, you will find lots of templates that you can use. Although it may be tempting to use a template that has many colors and designs, it is suggested that you stick to a simple template. The reason is that using a template that has so many designs may decrease the readability of your site. Also, a simple design makes the site look more professional. As for the color combination, it is suggested by many to have a go-to color (any color of your choice), and then combine it with one of the primary colors. It is also advised that you use the color gray since it has a touch of class and is often found in many professional and formal websites. Of course, these are not hard rules but mere suggestions. The design, layout, and color, of professional websites, vary depending on the style that you adapt. It is would be good to have someone to take a look at your website and ask for honest comments and suggestions. In designing your website, focus on making it more professional looking. Be sure that it will give to your website visitors the best experience possible.

Make your site mobile friendly

By now you should already know that increasing your SEO is not just about being concerned with Google search engine. You should also consider the quality of your site itself. Therefore, you should be sure that your site can easily be accessed using a mobile reason. The reason is that most, if not all, Internet users usually surf the web using their mobile phones. Make sure that your site is convenient to navigate on mobile as it is on a desktop computer. Also, check the pages and links, and make sure that they are all working properly.

Promotion

Promoting your site, or more specifically, the contents of your site is important. There are many services online that offer to promote your site for a fee; however, the problem here is that such services can be expensive. You can also find people who will promote your site at a low cost by visiting content mills and gig sites like Fiverr. However, the problem is that most of these promotions are of low quality. They normally offer to send more than fifty thousand traffic to your blog, but take note that such traffic is of low quality that comes from fake or bot accounts, many of which are merely computer-generated traffic.

The best way to promote your blog is simply to continue to update it with high-quality contents on a regular basis and promote these contents via social media. Let people who are really interested in the contents to like and share your stuff. This way, you can get good-quality traffic.

Build trust

This is a very important element of SEO and of any successful blog or website. As you may notice, the most successful sites are those that have the trust of so many people. But, building this trust is not as easy as it may seem. So, how do you develop this trust between you and your site visitors? Since you will not be meeting with them face to face and the only way that you connect with them is through your posts, the best and quickest way to build trust is by sharing useful and valuable information. This is also the reason why you are encouraged to come up with high-quality articles. If people learn from your posts and know that your articles can be trusted, they also get to trust the site itself, as well as the writer of its contents. Once trust is established, then it often leads to repeat visitors. And, of course, the more people who trust your website, the more referrals and re-shares you will get. As a result, your SEO rating will also increase.

Connect with influencers

Influencers are people who are considered as experts on a particular subject. As such, they have a strong influence. Just imagine how much you can benefit if you are able to connect with an influencer. The good news is that it is possible and that you can. So, how do you connect with influencers? Well, the first step is to identify who the influencers are. A good way to find out is by using BuzzStream. When you use BuzzStream, you will be given a list of influencers that belong to a particular niche. You can then message or connect with an influencer and ask him for a quote. If the influencer agrees, he will help you with your content, even with promoting it.

Not all influencers have a huge amount of following. However, they often have a high-quality following. This means that they may only have less than 500 connections, but their connections are those who will engage and even reshare relevant and helpful articles.

The key to an influencer is his inbox. Now, many people may not be aware of this, but it is fairly easy to message an influencer if you know the right place to connect with him. The secret lies in a social media platform that is for professionals. Yes, that is no other than LinkedIn. LinkedIn will allow you to connect with professionals, which includes influencers. Most influencer will accept it if you send them a request to be connected. Once connected, you can then send a message right into his inbox. Make sure that you send a polite and professional message, and make it compelling enough so that the influencer will not be able to ignore your message.

Use Google Plus

Although not required, joining and participating in Google Plus can be very beneficial to your SEO rating. But first, what is Google Plus? It is the social media platform of Google. It is similar to Facebook. When you use this, you will easily find a good amount of readership for your contents. What is more, these people can give your contents a +1, which is an effective way to recommend your site and your posts to Google. The more +1s you get, the higher is your chance to be on the first page of Google. The good news is that it is very easy to get +1s and even engagements when you use Google Plus. And, if you use Blogger as your site's platform, you can have the comments on Google Plus to appear on your blog or website.

Joining Google Plus is easy and free. It will only take less than five minutes to complete the signing up process. Another good thing about Google Plus is that it has many communities that you can join. You can take advantage of this and join those communities that are related to the subject of your blog. By doing so, you can be sure that the members of the community are interested in the topic of your website. Once you are a member of a community, you can start posting and sharing your posts with the community. Also, you are not limited to joining only a single community. Google Plus has many communities that cater to different interests. If you do not think the present communities are not a good match for your topic, then you are also free to create a new community.

It is also worth noting that many people on Google Plus are also writers, bloggers, and webmasters. By connecting with people and joining relevant communities, you can easily form mutual connections with other interesting people. It is not uncommon to find people on GooglePlus who would like, share, and comment, on every post that you make. Google Plus is a really nice place to promote your stuff. You will surely find like minded people in this social platform of Google itself.

Chapter 3
Common Mistakes and How to Avoid Them

In order to enjoy the best result of using SEO, you need to avoid the common mistakes that beginners often fall into. It is important that you become aware of these pitfalls so that you can make the necessary adjustments and not commit the same mistakes.

Keyword stuffing

Gone are the days when you can simply fill your contents with keywords and see your blog appear or the first page of Google. Although the use of keywords is important in SEO, stuffing your contents with keyword would be counterproductive. In fact, it is considered a bad practice that once Google detects that you merely stuff your articles with keywords, you can expect to are a drop in your SEO ranking. Never forget the recommended keyword density in order to avoid stuffing your articles with keywords. The recommended keyword density is 1% to 3%. It is also important to note that when you use keywords, you should not force them into the article. This means that although keywords are meant to be repeated in the article according to the right keyword density, they must come naturally and not ruin the smooth flow of the words in your article. Also, put more focus on giving useful information than repeating your keywords needlessly in an article.

Plagiarism

It is an unfortunate truth that plagiarism is rampant online. Many articles that you find online these days are just rewritten versions of other existing articles. Take note that another way to commit plagiarism is by claiming another person's idea as your own. Therefore, even if a particular article has passed online plagiarism checkers, such as Copyscape, it does not automatically mean that it can no longer be liable for plagiarism. Plagiarism is bad not only because it is considered a crime. It is also bad for your site's SEO. When Google finds out that you merely plagiarized or rewrite another person's contents, it will cause you to decrease your SEO rating and may stop recommending your site completely on its search engine page results.

Social media spamming

Although it is recommended that you promote your site on social media, you should only do so moderately. Some people bombard their followers with self-serving promotions, which is counterproductive. Avoid sending multiple promotions in a row. Otherwise, people may start unfollowing you. One to five promotional emails a day would be fine. Also, avoid sharing the same post over and over again.

Buying links

Since the use of inbound links has been effective in increasing a site's SEO ranking, there are services that offer link building for a fee. Take note that you should always avoid buying links no matter how persuasive is the offer. The reason is simple: Google's Webmaster Guidelines does not allow such practice. It is also worth noting that Google has a way to detect suspicious, unnatural, and manipulative links. This can result in getting a lower SEO ranking. Do not buy links. Instead, you should earn them. Of course, the best way to earn links is by publishing top-notch contents and by doing legitimate promotions.

Complicated keywords

When you come up with keywords that you will use for an article, you should keep in mind that the people who make a search online do not spend too much time thinking of the right keywords to use in the search bar. Most of the time, they just use the first thought that pops up in their mind. Also, they often use just simple words. Therefore, when you plan the keywords that you will be using, stick to simple words.

Buying website visitors and followers

As already mentioned, buying website visitors and followers is a practice that you should avoid. It is a waste of money. It is also disappointing to see a website or blog that has thousands of followers but with very little engagement. This is exactly what happens when you buy visitors and followers.

There are now many services that will offer you followers plus engagements for a limited time for a small fee. Now, although you will get engagements, you can expect to get low-quality engagements. These are like bot accounts that automatically reshare or like whatever you post. Even your real human followers might notice it. Take note that it is so much better to have few high-quality followers or connections than thousands of low-quality followers.

Not having a call to action message

People who search for answers or information online are very much open to suggestions. In fact, they are more focused on absorbing as much information that they can get than analyzing whatever that they read. Therefore, the key here is to offer high-quality articles and, at the same time, including a short and direct call to action message. If you are selling a product or service, then now is the time to include it in your post. You can also include links within your article, as we have already discussed. It is a good practice to keep your call to action message as short as possible, just around one or two sentences but make it clear.

Not using quality external links

When you share information, it is best to link it to the article where you got your source. This is also a good way to avoid plagiarism. Take note that when you cite your reference, you should use a site (if taken from another website) that is well established in the industry. This will help increase the credibility of your own article. Good sources are government websites or records, legitimate companies, hospitals, famous people or figures, and others.

Expecting for quick results

Building your SEO takes time. Even if you have five quality articles on your site, they would not be enough to place your homepage on the first page of Google — of course, it is still possible but the chances are slim. It also takes time to build readership and a good number of active followers. It is not uncommon for some articles to go viral on the Internet only after several months after you have published them on your site. When it comes to building your blog and SEO, you need to be patient and persevering. This is true especially during the first few months that you start working on your blog's SEO. The good news is that even though this may take some time, things will get easier to maintain once you achieve a good level of SEO. In fact, your site's traffic will grow on its own. But, before that, you need to work on building a good foundation, and that means exercising the best SEO practicing continuously.

Hiring low-quality ghostwriters

Most people who build a site or blog just for the sole purpose of earning money do not want to spend time researching and writing articles. Instead, they act as businessmen and hire ghostwriters to do the work for them. In order to save on cost, they look for ghostwriters whom they can pay at a cheap rate. You can find many of such writers from content mills. They would be willing to write articles for you for as low as $2.5 per article of 500 words. Now, this may seem like a good deal. In fact, many of these writers even claim to be good writers with an attractive writing background. However, you need to be careful about hiring such low-cost writers. The truth is that real professional ghostwriters know just how much their writing is really worth. Being offered a low amount of $2.5 per article would be an insult or a joke to them. Most, if not all, of the writers who accept a rate that is somewhere on the low end, cannot produce high-quality contents. If you get lucky and fool a good writer to accept a low rate, you cannot expect to work on your project for a long time since if he is really that good, then he will quickly realize that he deserves a much better rate.

There are people who hire multiple low-quality writers so that they can have lots of contents on their site within a short period of time. The problem here is not just the poor quality but also the voice of the articles. Since the articles are written by unprofessional ghostwriters, you can expect to have the articles written with diverse structures, flow, and format. Your readers will find out that they are reading works from different people, since the articles will not be written in a similar way. This applies even though you instruct your writers to follow a specific format, since the words themselves and the flow of the words would still be different from one another. Hence, when you hire ghostwriters, you should only work with professional ghostwriters. However, you can expect to have a much higher cost.

Link exchange sites

Avoid those free link exchange sites that will direct low-quality visitors to your site. Do not forget that Google is a top-notch search engine. Once it finds out that you "cheat" your site's traffic with low-quality link exchange sites like Traffup, you will be marked as a spam. Be careful of this because this may cause you to get removed from the page result. Hence, instead of wasting your time with low-quality traffic and link exchange sites which are only counterproductive, you should focus on creating useful contents.

Hidden text

Although hard to find, your competitors may beat you in the competition for hiding text. This hidden text usually exists in sites that already have other problems. Now, if Google or other search engines find it, then there is a risk that your site will be dropped off the list. Do not underestimate how Google works. For example, if your site accepts comments and reviews, and a reader writes some keywords in the comment box even if they have a wrong spelling, then it would still be okay. However, if you manipulate things yourself and be the one to write the same comments, then expect for Google to find out about such manipulation. In turn, you can also expect for your SEO rating to decrease. It is worth noting that Google does not act quickly on these matters. However, once Google drops you off the list or lowers your SEO rating, then it would be hard to make Google change its mind.

Another common way hidden text or invisible text is used is by typing keywords and giving it a font color the same as the background color. By doing so, you are able to have more keywords in your article, even though those words are not seen by your readers. It is merely a way to "cheat" the increase of a site's SEO through the use of keywords. Since the keywords have the same color as the background, people will not see them. The problem is that this is considered an unfair and deceptive practice. Although this may work for some time, once Google finds out about it, it can cause a serious decline in your SEO rating. In fact, Google may even cause your site to be removed from its SERP. AS you can see, using black hat SEO has its short-term advantages, but once Google catches up (and it will), the consequences can be severe.

Using the same content on another blog

Some people use the very same article on another blog that he owns thinking that since both blogs belong to him he has a right to post the same article on both blogs. Yes, of course, you have the right to do so. However, Google will see it as a duplicate content — which, in fact, it really is — and Google hates duplicate contents, including rewritten contents. Therefore, producing the same article on another blog would be counterproductive. Instead, what you can do is to share a link to the original post. After all, sharing links is allowed.

Using Flash

There is nothing wrong with using Flash. However, Flash may take time to load, especially if the net connection is not that strong. People also do not have the patience to wait for it to load and work. As for SEO, Flash does not give Google or any search engine any help or assistance to increase a site's SEO. The reason is that Google cannot understand whatever it is in your Flash presentation. What search engines need is text. The more quality texts you have, the better. Now, in case that you really want to use Flash, then just be sure to use HTML on the page so that Google can have something to read and relate to.

Clickbait

As the term implies, clickbait is where you offer something that is intriguing and interesting, but once a person clicks on it, he will be taken to a site that has no relation to the "bait." For example, *Click here and find out the best ways to make money online.* However, when you click on the link, you will be taken to a site that is about fashion or bodybuilding. Simply put, what is offered is different from what is actually given. Although this can drive traffic to your site, especially if you use a catchy bait, it is can be hurtful to your SEO ranking. Again, Google punishes those who cheat their way to SEO success.

Low-quality page

Take note that this does not just refer to the article but to the whole page itself. But, constitutes a low-quality page? Well, it is simply the opposite of following the best strategies and practices of SEO. Therefore, a page is considered of low quality if the contents are poorly written, or if the contents do not share anything valuable. Also, the page must be easy to navigate, and it should be professionally designed. Of course, the contents must also observe the proper use of keywords. When considering the quality of a page, you should look at the page as a whole and be sure that every part of the whole achieves a good purpose.

Make-money site

It is true that many people who want to learn SEO want to master it because they intend to use it to make money online. Now, it must be clear that using your site to make money is not bad. In fact, Google itself supports such websites that it even offers Google ads so that you can earn a decent amount of income. Not to mention, there are bloggers who earn a full-time income simply by displaying Google ads on their blogs. However, what is considered a bad practice is when your site is only about making you earn money without offering any value to its visitors.

Always remember that Google places importance on value. Your site or blog should always give value to something and not just have self-serving contents that will make you earn money. Without sharing value on your site, you can never expect Google to give you a high SEO rating. In fact, when Google finds out that you are only up for the money, it can lower your current SEO rating or even remove it completely from its index.

Improper use of bold and italics

Some people follow the practice of formatting their keywords in bold or italics thinking that it will make the keywords more visible to search engine bots. There is no proof that this works. Also, this is an irregular and wrong use of such format. As you already know, Google does not like undue manipulation. Therefore, it is best if you do not apply this kind of practice. Otherwise, when Google finds out about it, you may be punished severely. Only use bold and italics when they are needed, and never use them for the purpose of SEO.

Chapter 4
Best Practices

To help turn the odds in your favor, you should also know and apply certain practices that can further boost the SEO rating of your site. These practices are observed by the top bloggers and webmasters. May these practices help you and guide your way to success. It is important that you turn these practices into a habit so that you can enjoy the benefits of a successful blog or website.

Consider the competition

The strengths and weaknesses of your site are relative. They are dependent upon the strengths and weaknesses of your competitors. Therefore, you need to consider and study your competitors. A good way to do this is by visiting and analyzing their website. Pay attention to how their posts are constructed, the keywords that they use, as well as the overall layout and performance of their site. You can then compare the strengths and weaknesses of your own site with the strengths and weaknesses of your competitors. Aim to work on your weaknesses. Try to turn them into strength. Of course, you will have to make adjustments in the process. As you work on your weaknesses, you should not forget to also maintain your strengths. In fact, you should strive to further strengthen your strengths. By doing so, the competition will help turn your site into the best site that it can ever be.

Many people shy away from competition. This is wrong. After all, there will always be competition. But, do not let your competitors discourage you from building a well-established blog. Instead, learn from your competitors, and focus on building the best site possible. Take note that SEO is not just about using the right keywords. It is also about getting ahead of the competition.

Fill in the gaps in your niche

As you examine the competitors that you have in your niche, you should also look for gaps in your niche. These gaps refer to the topics or subtopics that your competitors have failed to tackle in their articles. Take note that these gaps can be the goldmine that you are looking for. Things that have not yet been covered are hot topics. Imagine all the people who look for that particular article will end up in your website. But, of course, it is not easy to spot this kind of goldmine, but it is still possible. The best way to do this is by shifting your perspective. Remember that many unique articles can be written regarding the same subject matter. All that you need is to change the perspective on the subject. Be creative and do not be afraid to experiment.

Always be kind and polite

Although this advice has no direct relation to your site's SEO, this is important to keep your SEO rating high, as well as to possible increase your current SEO rating. Take note that the more people are fond of your site, the better your site will rank. This, of course, is still part of SEO. One of the effective ways to make your visitors be more interested in your site is to make them interested in the author of the site or blog — and that person is you. Be kind and polite at all times, especially when you respond to the comments on your blog.

It is not uncommon to encounter harsh and rude comments. Generally, there are two reasons why you may get bad and insulting comments on your site. One reason is when you post an article of low quality. People may feel as if you have wasted their time with your poorly written article, and so they leave you a negative comment. The other reason is that some people simply want to write something bad for no good reason. Now, when you get a bad review or comment, you need to relax and analyze the situation. Ask yourself if there is a good reason behind the negative comment. If, for example, it is true that the comment is reasonable, then be flexible and open enough to make the necessary adjustments. Also, do not forget to thank your reader for helping you make your site better. However, if it appears that the comment was made simply to harass or just to write something bad for no good reason, then it is better to just ignore it or answer it back politely. To be safe, just ignore it and pay more attention to those comments that are honest and true.

Proper length of article

There is no clear-cut rule on how long an article should be. However, on average, an article may range from 500 to 1,000 words. It is good to avoid writing shorter articles because they tend to lack sufficient information. Longer articles are also not strongly recommended because they tend to send potential readers away. The reason is that many people who make a search online want answers quickly. They do not want to read a long article just to find out why SEO is important for one's website. They want the answers as fast as possible.

Of course, this rule is not absolute. You can, from time to time, exceed the word count of 1,000 per article. There are many successful blogs that even reach more than 2,000 in a single post. However, when you do so, be sure to observe the proper keyword count, and be sure that the article still has a high quality. Unfortunately, some people come up with long posts when they can, in fact, share the same information in less than 500 words. The thing is that when you make a long write-up, it should be because there are many important information that you need to share that cannot be summarized clearly in just 500 or 1,000 words. Be as concise as possible. Do not write a 2,000-word article when you can do it in 500 words.

Conversational tone

If you manage a blog, the recommended practice is to write in a conversational tone. The reason is that people get to understand things more easily if it is written in ordinary language, without metaphors or hard-to-understand jargons. Now, this does not mean that you should write as if you are just talking to a person. The writing still needs to be concise without wasting any line or word. Of course, this is a matter of personal preference. You can take a different tone if you want. However, it is suggested that people like a tone that is relaxed and comfortable. Something that is direct and easy to understand.

Update your site regularly

Did you know that search engines like Google recommend the latest posts on a specific subject? Yes, they want the freshest write-up. After all, why would you read an old version when the latest and updated version on the same subject is available? Therefore, updating your site regularly is an important part of your overall SEO strategy. This is also a good way to keep your current readership interested in your site. But, of course, this does not mean that you can just update it with random articles. The practice remains the same: You should update your site with high-quality articles — and articles that your readers will find useful and interesting.

Grow your followers

Take note that this refers to high-quality followers. The more followers you have the more people will read your posts and it can also increase the number of reshares on your article. A good thing about getting other people to share your contents is that you can get to tap a new network of people. When a person shares your content on social media, the article gets shared with all the people in his network. Now, if one or several people from his network get to like your article and also reshares it with their own network — so and so forth — just imagine how much traffic to your site this can generate. In fact, this is how contents become viral on the Internet.

This is another reason why you should have an email list or newsletter on your site that people can subscribe to with just a click of a mouse. Having an email list will notify your subscribers every time you post something new on your blog. Yes, this does not increase your SEO ranking but it will help keep your current readership. Take note that you should take care of your current website visitors or readers. A decrease in website visitors can have a negative impact on your SEO rating. After all, why would Google recommend your site if only a few people want to follow it?

How do you make people subscribe to your email list? The thing is that you do not force anyone to subscribe to your email list. Rather, you just need to put an option to subscribe to your email list somewhere on your site where people can see it. People will subscribe to your email list if they like your contents. Again, having high-quality contents is the key to get people to subscribe to your email list and newsletter. For this to happen, they need to trust you. To earn their trust, you need to provide them with helpful and informative contents. If they like what you offer them, then there is a good chance that they will sign up or subscribe so that they can follow your site. Take note that they only subscribe when they think that it is for their own advantage, and not because they want to support your site. How can they think that it is for their own advantage? Well, again, they must feel that they need to read whatever is on your site. If they think that your posts can help them and give them the information that they need, then they will subscribe on their own. In fact, they might even sign up for your newsletter.

Proper timing

Proper timing is also essential. You should be able to identify the time when most of your connections are active online. This is the time that you should use to post new contents on your blog. Take note that the more engagements your articles get, the more chances they will spread and help increase your SEO rating. Now, it is safe to assume that your connections and readership can be found all over the world. Therefore, finding the most opportunistic time to publish a new post may need some trial and error. To do this, simply publish your contents at different hours. Pay attention to how active are your connections, and choose the time when your followers are most active to engage with your posts. You can also try to check the profile of your high-quality (active) connections and see the usual time that they upload a new post. The important part here is to be able to know the best time to publish a new post. Again, this is a matter of trial and error. It is also worth noting that your connections will grow. Therefore, the best time to publish a post may vary. Now, some other bloggers publish at the same time of the day and make it a custom practice. The reason is so that readers can safely have something to expect. For example, a new post will be made every Sunday at 8 AM (New York City time zone). This, of course, is a matter of personal preference. Some other authors and bloggers do not like this approach because they feel like they are being forced to publish something even when they have nothing good to share with the world. Again, there is no hard and fast rule on this matter. Either way, has pros and cons of its own. This is something that you decide for yourself.

Value over profit

You should give more emphasis on creating value for your customers or visitors than the profit that you can get. If you focus solely on making a profit, people will find it hard to trust your site. But, if you focus on creating value, people will be more open to you, even to the products and services that you may offer.

Get updated

Google's algorithm continues to be developed. make sure that you are updated on any relevant news about Google's special algorithm. For example, before, the use of keywords alone can take you on the front page of Google provided you have a good number of quantity on your site. However, today, this keywords and quantity alone are no longer enough. You also need high-quality contents. Make sure to keep your eye on Google's developments, and be ready to act accordingly.

Divide long paragraphs

Reading on the computer or any other device is different from reading a physical book. The eyes are more strained when you read on a device. For this reason, you should make some adjustment to make the reading experience more comfortable for your readers. According to various studies, the eyes get more strained to read a whole block of texts on a computer. Therefore, to help increase your article's readability, you should divide a long paragraph into short paragraphs. This way, it will be easier to read. Also, people tend to shy away from posts that are composed of big blocks of texts. Keep the layout of your article clean and easy on the eyes.

Focus on building a quality website

Some people get too caught up with SEO and fail to realize that SEO is only part of the game. After all, even if you master all the SEO strategies in the world, it will still not be enough to get your site on the first page of Google. The reason is that SEO can only work if you have something valuable to share. Therefore, focus on building a quality website. This means that you should focus on creating a place online that can help people and can give the best user experience. If you have a good product or service that you can offer, then SEO will come easily. However, if you only have low-quality articles to share, then you cannot expect any positive outcome despite all the serious SEO strategies and efforts that you do.

Quality user experience

The best SEO practitioners know that true SEO is not just about the use of keywords. To rank well on Google search engine result pages, your visitors must be given the best quality of experience. To dominate Google, you should not rely on manipulation or unfair tactics. Instead, you should focus on providing quality offerings. The quality that is demanded today is much higher than years ago. Google continuously improves itself and ensures to offer only the best to its clients.

Take note that quality is not just limited to the contents posted on your site, but it also includes the whole site itself, such as its design, performance, speed, and layout, among others.

Chapter 5
Putting It All Together

Now that you have a good foundation of SEO, it is time to put everything together and use what you know to boost your site's SEO rating. The way successful SEO practitioners and bloggers do it actually follows a steady routine. Of course, all of the best practices should be applied all throughout, and you also need to watch out for the pitfalls that you may encounter along the way.

This chapter will guide you on how to get things together and apply them at the same time. By now, you are expected to have a good and working website with some contents on it. Perhaps you also have a few followers — if none, then do not worry.

So, the first step is to come up with an idea for your next article. Now, do not just make this any idea. Instead, think about what you think people who are interested in your subject would like to read. Consider what your market *wants* to read. If it is something that you know really well, then you can proceed to write the article. However, if it is something that you do not know completely, then it is time for you to do a research on it. When you do a research, be sure to check more than five different websites and draw your own understanding or conclusion. Take note that you should not duplicate the contents of other websites. Duplicating content is a part of black hat SEO; therefore, you should always avoid it.

Write possible keywords for your next article. Make a list of at least five different keywords. If you want, you can use Google keyword planner to help you come up with good keyword phrases. Be sure to use long-tail keywords. Pick the best long-tail keywords on your list and use them for your next article.

The next step is to write a list of at least five titles for your next article.Make them as compelling as possible. Do not forget to include your keywords in your title. You then choose the title that you think is best among the others. The next step is now to write at least a 500-word article about your chosen topic. Do not rush the writing process. In fact, you are given three days to finish this article. When done, let the article sit still for a moment. Do not even look at it, and do not publish it yet. The next day, you should edit your article. Pay attention to any grammar and punctuation errors. You should also read your article out loud to know if the lines flow smoothly and naturally. Again, leave the article for a while. After about five hours, have another round of editing. Remove redundant lines and words in the article. If there are changes that you can make to come up with a better article, then do not hesitate to do it.

Make sure that the article is as good as you can make it just before you publish it. Take note that there is no rush to publishing your work.After all, once you publish your article, it will be there forever, unless you decide to put it down. if you are already happy with your article, and you do not know any other way to make it better, then it is time for you to publish it.

However, before you publish your article, decide if you want to use an image or not. If you are going to use an image, be sure that you have the permission to use it. To be safe, stick to public domain images and those images that you have taken yourself. Take note that if the image is not of public domain, then you need to get the permission of the owner of the image before you can use it. Do not worry; there are many public domain images online that you can use. It is a good practice to include one or two pictures per post of a normal length of 500 to 1,000 words (per article).Remember that when you use an image, then you should also add ALT text so that Google will be able to understand the image that you are using.

Now, it is time to publish your article. If you want, you can give it another go of editing. You may choose the time that you think is best to publish your article. At any time that you are ready, just click the publish button. Right after publishing, check if the published version is the way that you expect it. Pay attention to the format and if the proper spacing is observed. Also, check the links if they are working properly, if any.

The next step is to promote your new post on social media. If you are also using Google Plus, then it is also the time to share your content with the community. Before you post something on Google Plus community, be sure to read and follow the posting guidelines. How you promote your post on social media also matters. It is recommended that you use a catchy image. As they say, pictures speak more than a thousand words. Also, many people do not like to view anything that is full of texts. The sight makes it appear like a heavy reading, which tends to keep people away. Together with the picture, it is suggested that you include an interesting line to catch the attention and interest of anyone who reads it. It is good to keep this short, about one to three sentences only. of course, you should have a clickable link that leads to the full article on your site.

You can expect to get comments and engagements. Be sure to answer every comment. Yes, you read that right. Reply to all the comments, except maybe those negative comments that have no basis. If you do not reply or only reply to some, it would be unfair to other people who also commented. This may tell them not to comment anymore next time. Do not make your readers feel like they are being ignored. It does not matter if your reply takes more than a week. The important point is that you do not ignore the people who commented. Of course, it is best if you can reply to all the comments within 24 hours, or as early as possible.

You might be wondering why it is recommended to answer to all the comments when, in fact, there are popular writers who do not even bother to reply to all comments on their site. Well, the point is that those people are famous. And, even if they do not respond, the world will understand them because they often get hundreds, if not thousands, of engagements per post that it is almost impossible for them to reply to all comments. The strategy that is explained here takes assumes that you are not yet as famous as those top-notched authors and bloggers. After all, if you are already as famous as they are, then you probably do not have to worry anymore about SEO.

After sharing your work and replying to all engagements, do not forget to also comment on other people's posts. In the online world, you usually get the treatment that you extend to others. For example, if you comment on other people's posts, there is a good chance that they will also comment back on your posts. It is a give and share process.

Again, repeat the steps from the start and think of another idea for your next article. As you can see, there is really no secret to SEO success. It is all a matter of hard work, dedication, and perseverance. Those who give up early fail to see the effects of SEO, while those persevere and continue to practice the best SEO practices for a long term get the opportunity to reap the rewards of their hard work. And, as usual, providing high quality should always be your priority. As you know by now, the strategies and best practices should all be a natural part of your day-to-day life. SEO does not happen or end overnight. It is a lifelong process without end. So, never give up. Continue to turn your blog or website into the best site that it can ever be, and you will soon find your blog on the first page of Google search engine result pages.

Although Google keeps on updating its special algorithm to ensure the best service and some SEO techniques may even be affected in the process, the basics of SEO such as always providing high-quality contents and making sure that your site is professionally structured and designed will never change. As long as to stick to these basics, then you can be sure to be on the right path to SEO success. It is important that you make these things a part of your day-to-day activity. After all, SEO should be an important part of your website. It is an important ingredient to your success.

Conclusion

Thanks for making it through to the end of this book. We hope it was informative and able to provide you with all of the tools you need to achieve your goals whatever they may be.

The next step is to apply everything that you have learned and get your website to have a higher SEO ranking. It is time to dominate Google, be on the first page of search engine result pages, and drive more traffic to your site.